THE
HEALING POWER OF CHOCOLATE

Writer
Carol Turkington

Consultant
Diane L. McKay, Ph.D., F.A.C.N.

Publications International, Ltd.

Cover Photo: Digital Vision

Writer:

Carol Turkington is a medical writer, editor, and consultant with a degree in journalism, 28 years of experience at newspapers in New York and Massachusetts, three years as a medical writer/editor at Duke University Medical Center, and five years as a senior writer in clinical psychology and biobehavioral medicine for the American Psychological Association in Washington, D.C. She has written health articles for national magazines including *Vogue, Parents, American Baby, Psychology Today, Discovery Channel Magazine, Good Housekeeping, Redbook, Self,* and *USA Weekend.* She has also written more than 50 popular nonfiction books, covering child and parenting issues, women's issues, nutrition, and general and mental health.

Consultant:

Diane L. McKay, Ph.D., F.A.C.N., is a scientist in the Antioxidants Research Laboratory at the Jean Mayer USDA Human Nutrition Research Center on Aging at Tufts University and an adjunct assistant professor at Tufts University's Friedman School of Nutrition Science and Policy in Boston. She is a member of the American Society for Nutrition and a fellow of the American College of Nutrition.

Table of Contents

Chocolate News to Savor

It's the very definition of good news: Chocolate may be good for you! And this book is where you'll read all about it.

Since ancient times, chocolate has been far more than a guilty pleasure. It's functioned as medicine, sacred ceremonial beverage, status symbol, even money. To give you a taste of the value that previous civilizations placed on chocolate, the first chapter traces the surprisingly rich history of this delectable treasure. The second chapter unwraps the process of making chocolate, from its roots in the cacao tree through the technological advances that have brought us the many varieties of chocolate available today. And the last chapter explores the latest research that suggests cacao-rich chocolate may act on blood vessels, blood pressure, and circulation to lower heart-disease and stroke risk; improve blood-sugar control in those with diabetes; and supply powerful antioxidants to help protect cells from damage that can lead to cancer and certain dementias, including Alzheimer's disease. The final chapter also explains how to select and enjoy chocolate to maximize its healing potential while minimizing the risk of weight gain.

It's the news chocolate-lovers everywhere have been waiting for. So read on, and enjoy. Healing has never tasted so good.

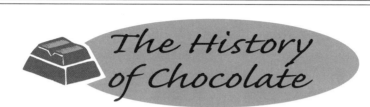

The History of Chocolate

From its earliest cultivation in ancient Mexico and Central America, through its journeys across the Atlantic, to the present, chocolate has been treasured. Yet for most of that history, chocolate little resembled the smooth, sweet confection cherished today. And the roles it played in bygone days—from nourishing beverage and sacred liquid to status symbol, money, and medicine—gave it an importance that far surpasses its status among even the most devoted modern "chocoholics."

Chocolate is made from the seeds of the fruit of the cacao tree. The seemingly inedible, almond-size seeds, which are surrounded by sweet, tangy pulp, develop inside seed pods. The seed pods resemble footballs and grow out from the tree's trunk. The cacao tree is native to the tropical rainforests of Mesoamerica—the ancient region that covered the southern and eastern portions of Mexico, Guatemala, Belize, and parts of El Salvador and Honduras. The area was home to numerous, remarkably advanced civilizations prior to its conquest by Europeans.

No one knows for sure which of the Mesoamericans first came up with the idea of using cacao seeds to produce something edible. No decipherable written records exist from the earliest groups in the region. Evidence does show that the Maya, whose culture was at its heyday from A.D. 250 to 900 (referred to as the Classic Maya period), typically used cacao seeds to make a thick, bitter chocolate beverage. It is the Maya, therefore, who often get credit as the inventors of chocolate. Yet some experts suspect that chocolate-drinking actually originated far earlier, around 1000 B.C., probably with the Olmec, who dominated the muggy lowlands of Mexico's Gulf Coast from about 1500 to 400 B.C. (The Gulf Coast forests provide ideal habitat for the cacao tree, which requires consistently warm  temperatures, high humidity, and plenty of rain.) Indeed, *cacao,* the Mayan name for the tree and for chocolate, likely comes from the word *kakawa,* which was the name of the tree in the language spoken by the Olmec. Whether it was the Olmec or the Maya who first discovered chocolate, however, it is the evidence from the Mayan civilization (and from the Aztecs who followed) that provides insight into how chocolate was gathered, made, and used and how highly it was valued in Mesoamerica.

Classic Mayan Chocolate

The Classic Maya harvested the seeds—or beans—from cacao trees, fermented and dried them, roasted them, removed their shells, and ground them into paste. (Much of that process remains unchanged to this day.) They often combined this paste with water, cornmeal, chili peppers, and other spices, then poured the spicy, bitter mixture back and forth between two containers to create a frothy head (a very popular feature). This nutritious drink seems to have been the most common Mayan method of consuming chocolate. The elite would savor it at the end of a meal, much as modern diners might have a bit of brandy or port. (Cacao paste was probably added to corn gruel and consumed in other ways, too, but there is little surviving evidence to inform us about these uses.)

Although chocolate was clearly a favorite of Mayan royals and priests, commoners likely enjoyed the drink on at least some occasions, as well. Many ancient Mayan artifacts are decorated with paintings of the people gathering, preparing, or drinking cacao. It appears to have been a truly integral part of their religious and social lives.

An Ancient Healer

Mesoamericans considered chocolate a restorative medicine that could fight fatigue, cool fevers, and strengthen those "weak of heart." It was even issued to soldiers to fortify them during battle.

The cacao bean and beverage were used in a variety of religious rituals honoring the Mayan gods—the liquid chocolate sometimes standing in for blood—and were considered "god food." The Maya even had a god of cacao. In the tombs of their deceased rulers, they included cacao beans and various vessels and utensils associated with cacao consumption. The chocolate drink was also exchanged between bride and groom during the traditional marriage ceremony. And in pre-conquest Mayan baptismal rites, ground cacao beans mixed with ground flowers and pure water from tree hollows was used to anoint little Mayan boys and girls.

The Maya were so fond of chocolate that they not only gathered cacao beans in the forests, they learned to grow the trees in their gardens. Even Mayan groups living in the Yucatán, where the climate wouldn't support a tropical rainforest, apparently found ways to grow some cacao trees. The Maya also had extensive trade networks that helped ensure steady supplies of cacao throughout Mesoamerica, even in areas too cool or dry for cacao trees to thrive.

The Aztec Take on Chocolate

Sometime after A.D. 1200, another group of ancient Mesoamericans, the Aztec, migrated from western Mexico to the cities in the central valley and went on to conquer many of the areas previously ruled by the Maya and other groups. From the resident Maya, the Aztec learned how to produce and prepare chocolate—and they learned to value it immensely, as well. But in their new arid home in central Mexico—the seat of their vast empire—they could not grow cacao trees. So the Aztec rulers began demanding cacao beans as tribute from the peoples they conquered. Aztec merchants also plied their extensive trade routes to purchase the beans from lowland Mayan areas outside their own empire.

For the Aztec, too, cacao had deep religious and symbolic meaning. They attributed its discovery to the Aztec god Quetzalcoatl. According to one of their myths, the Aztec received cacao when Quetzalcoatl descended from heaven on the beam of a morning star, carrying a cacao tree stolen from paradise. The Aztec, in turn, made offerings of cacao beans to their gods and used the chocolate drink—which they called *cacahuatl,* for "cacao water"—as a ceremonial beverage.

The Aztec loved cold chocolate drinks (unlike the Maya, who preferred theirs warm), but in the far more rigid Aztec communities, only special individuals—rulers, priests, great warriors, leading merchants, and honored guests—were officially allowed access to this beverage. The Aztec valued cacao even above silver and gold and believed wisdom and power came from consuming it.

In time, cacao became so highly prized in Aztec society that the beans themselves were used as money. They could buy clothes, food, and other supplies. The elite continued to enjoy their chocolate beverages, of course, but the poor were far more likely to use their few, precious beans to buy food and other necessities.

Blood of the Earth

It might not seem an appetizing comparison today, but the ancient Aztec viewed chocolate as the blood of the earth, to which they had a sacred bond. Scenes of Aztec gods piercing their ears and spilling their blood over cacao pods appear frequently on artifacts from the period. And evidence suggests ritualistic human and animal bloodletting took place on cacao plantations during Aztec festivals to honor their gods.

Enter the Spanish

It was only a matter of time before the secret of cacao spread beyond the Mesoamericans, and that journey began with the Spanish conquests in the New World. Christopher Columbus may have been the first Old World explorer to come across cacao beans. In his fourth and final voyage to the New World,

Columbus, along with his son Ferdinand and their crew, happened upon Mayan traders in two large canoes. As was their habit, the Spaniards captured one of the canoes to get a look at the kinds of goods that were traded and valued in this new land. Among the canoe's contents were fine clothes, weapons, even a copper bell, as well as a large number of unfamiliar beans. Columbus showed no interest in a load of what to him seemed worthless beans, but Ferdinand did note that when any of these beans fell to the ground, the natives would scramble to retrieve each one "as if an eye had fallen" from their heads. Columbus didn't bother bringing any of these strange beans back to Europe.

The true introduction of cacao to the Spanish invaders most likely came in 1519, when conquistador Hernán Cortés landed on the Yucatán Peninsula and met the Yucatán Maya. Like Columbus, Cortés was unimpressed by the beans, at least at first. He was far happier with the exotic treasures he found when he marched west, defeated the great Aztec ruler Montezuma, and conquered the Aztec capital of Tenochtitlan in 1521.

At the time, Tenochtitlan was the largest city in the world, and it was crammed with the bounty of a vast and powerful empire. In addition to the gold and

Chocolate as Aphrodisiac

Legend has it that the Aztec emperor Montezuma considered chocolate to be an aphrodisiac and drank up to 50 cups a day from golden goblets. At various times throughout its ensuing history, chocolate was promoted for this supposed benefit, although there is no scientific evidence to support such a link.

other riches Cortés craved, he found enormous stores of cacao beans. Indeed, there may have been as many as a *billion* cacao beans in the royal treasury at one time.

While Cortés found the chocolate beverage of the natives nearly undrinkable, he and his fellow invaders could not help but recognize the value the beans had among the Mesoamericans. As the Spanish conquerors took over as rulers and Spanish colonists began living among and marrying the natives, the traditional Mesoamerican uses of cacao were adopted or adapted by the Spanish settlers. They continued to use the beans as money for everyday purchases. But they found ways to make the chocolate drink more to their liking by warming it and adding spices and sweeteners with which they were more familiar. The Spaniards also came up with their own name for this warm cacao beverage, one that was easier for them to pronounce: chocolate. (There is disagreement over the exact origins of this word, but one strong theory is that it came from combining the Yucatec word for hot, *chocol,* and the Aztec word for water, *atl,* to form *chocolatl,* which the Spanish invaders would have pronounced *chocolaté.*)

Cacao Sails to Spain

While the Spanish explorers who conquered Mesoamerica in the early 1500s were likely the first Europeans to be introduced to chocolate, it is believed that the first chocolate to reach the Old World arrived in 1544. In that year, Dominican friars, who had traveled to the New World to convert the natives to Christianity, purportedly took a delegation of Mayan nobles from Guatemala back home to Spain to meet

Bitter Chapters in Chocolate's History

Chocolate is known for the pleasure it brings. But ironically, its very popularity in times past gave greedy men an excuse to inflict incredible cruelty and suffering on their fellow man.

Growing and harvesting cacao has always been a labor-intensive process. When the Spanish first conquered Mesoamerica, they forced the natives to do the work for them. In time, however, as chocolate became all the rage back in Europe, demand began to outstrip what the Mesoamericans could produce. In addition, the native population was in decline, largely as a result of diseases introduced by the European invaders. So Spain and other European countries began establishing cacao plantations in other conquered tropical nations, and to work these plantations, they brought in African slaves.

with Prince Philip (Philip II). The delegation brought with them the most valuable items from their culture, including gift jars of beaten cocoa, mixed and ready to drink.

The Spanish nobility quickly took to this new and exciting beverage, as did Catholic priests in Spain, who used the high-energy drink to sustain themselves during religious fasts. But it seems the Spanish wanted to keep the chocolate discovery from the rest of Europe. For close to a century, Spain hid the secret of the cacao beans, restricting their processing exclusively to monks hidden away in Spanish monasteries. Indeed, the secret was so well kept that when English pirates boarded what they thought was a Spanish treasure ship in 1579, they mistook its huge cache of cacao beans for a worthless load of dried sheep's droppings. In frustration, the pirates torched the whole ship, not realizing that they were destroying a cacao trove that would eventually be worth a king's ransom in their homeland.

As the drink became more and more popular among upper-crust Spaniards, it developed into a profitable industry for Spain, which began planting the cacao trees in its overseas colonies. As a result, Spain also became home to the very first chocolate factories, where the dried, fermented beans shipped from the New World were roasted and ground.

Eventually, with the decline of Spain as a world power, the secret of cacao leaked out, and the Spanish Crown's monopoly over the chocolate trade came to an end. By the mid-17th century, the knowledge of cacao had spread like wildfire to Italy, France, Germany, and England.

A Contagious Remedy

Much of chocolate's early popularity and viral-like spread through Europe can be traced to its use as a medicine. That's right! Chocolate, so often seen as unhealthy today, was originally promoted in Europe as a healing tonic. And in those days, folks were always on the lookout for anything that might help prevent or cure disease. It was, after all, a time before the modern understanding of disease and the effective treatments that followed. European medicine was still mired in the medical theories and practices of the Classical Greeks. This system, handed down from the likes of Hippocrates and Galen, held that disease resulted from imbalances in four substances, called humors, found naturally in the human body. These substances were phlegm, blood, yellow bile, and black

Chocolate Etiquette

During the 1600s, as chocolate made the rounds of the European upper classes, an entire protocol dictating the "proper" way to drink chocolate emerged. Along with it, a profitable industry developed to design silver and porcelain serving pieces and special cups for the taking of chocolate. The elaborate trappings and rituals of chocolate-drinking can even be seen in paintings from that era (known historically as the baroque period).

bile, and each was classified as either hot or cold, moist or dry. To keep the humors in balance or to remedy the imbalances thought to cause disease, a person would need to eat foods or take medicines that were likewise considered inherently hot or cold, wet or dry. These ancient theories about health and disease would eventually be disproved, of course, but in the meantime, the nutritious, energizing drink from the New World was assigned various attributes (although physicians of the time often disagreed about what these were) that made it seem beneficial for restoring and maintaining humoral balance.

In 1570, the royal physician to Philip II, the ruler of Spain, actually recommended chocolate to his majesty for, among other things, reducing fevers and easing stomach discomforts. As chocolate spread through Europe, physicians of the time chimed in with a variety of chocolate prescriptions. Over the next few hundred years, chocolate would be tested or prescribed for more than 100 different medicinal uses, from stimulating the nervous system and improving digestion and bowel function to treating health problems ranging from anemia and poor appetite to mental fatigue, poor breast-milk production, tuberculosis, fever, gout, kidney stones, and poor sexual appetite. While the cacao beans and the chocolate drink were most often prescribed as internal treatments, some doctors also made special topical preparations containing cacao beans, cacao bark, cacao butter, and even the leaves and flowers of the cacao tree to treat burns, cuts, and skin irritations.

From Treatment to Treat, European-Style

While its purported health-preserving and curative powers had much to do with the initial enthusiasm for chocolate in countries across Europe, its new and unique flavor and unheard-of energizing effects (chocolate arrived in Europe at about the same time as coffee and tea, giving Europeans their first experience of the stimulating effects of caffeine) no doubt helped to make it a much-craved mainstay among Europe's elite. Gradually, chocolate was transformed from medicine to luxury drink, with each country developing chocolate-drinking preferences, rituals, and accessories and adding unique flavorings to suit local tastes. The chocolate beverage from Mesoamerica took on an international flair, with the Spanish adding cinnamon and vanilla;

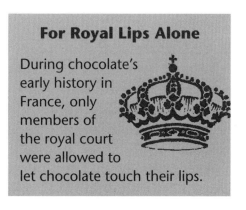

For Royal Lips Alone

During chocolate's early history in France, only members of the royal court were allowed to let chocolate touch their lips.

the Italians experimenting with perfumed flavors such as ambergris, musk, lemon peel, and even jasmine; and the French contributing cloves—and a lot more sugar.

Across Channel and "Pond"

The drink that so captivated continental Europeans made its way across the English Channel by 1650. But the English viewed all the exotic ingredients added to chocolate in Spain, Italy, and France as excessive. Instead, they added water to small amounts of chocolate, sometimes mixing in milk, eggs, sherry, port wine, and orange blossoms, as well. The growing popularity of the drink led to the opening of the first "chocolate house"—The Coffee Mill and Tobacco Roll—in London in 1657. Patterned after the coffeehouses of the day, chocolate houses provided a place for people (mostly men and, because chocolate went for 15 shillings a pound, mostly the wealthy) to sip chocolate, smoke tobacco, conduct business, talk politics, and even gamble.

Chocolate in England was produced primarily by Quakers, who gradually developed a near monopoly over chocolate-making in the British Empire. Fry, Cadbury, and Rowntree are probably the best known of these early Quaker chocolate makers. Because of their religious beliefs, Quakers were barred from many typical business activities, but they were allowed to turn their hands to food-related trades. Viewing bread in its biblical role as the "staff of life," the Quakers became great bakers, and soon they were adding chocolate to their cakes, cookies, and pies.

As Quakers and other colonists began to seek freedom in the New World, they brought with them their knowledge of how to produce chocolate. Chocolate reached the American colonies from England by the mid-1700s, and in no time, New England ship captains began filling their cargo holds with cacao beans from the tropics to supply this new market.

In the colonies, anyone with the cash to pay for it was allowed to drink chocolate, but in effect, it remained as it had been for most of its history—a luxury beverage for the wealthy. Thomas Jefferson, for example, fell in love with the chocolate drink when he was ambassador to France and began importing cacao beans and chocolate to Monticello. That exclusivity would finally change for good, however, with the coming of the Industrial Revolution, which sparked the transformation of chocolate into a milder-tasting solid confection and finally put it in the hands of the masses. The masses, in turn, embraced chocolate and began a love affair that continues in the Western world to this day.

From Elite Beverage to Everyman's Candy Bar

Even before the turn of the 19th century, there were "factories" dedicated to grinding cacao beans into a paste that could be formed into wafers or small cakes. These cakes, in turn, could be mixed with water to make chocolate. This liquid chocolate, however, was a far cry from the smooth, creamy cocoa, or hot chocolate, we drink today. The paste did not mix well with the water, so it produced a thick, gritty beverage that still retained much of the bitter taste of the cacao from which it was made. What's more, every step of the chocolate-making process was still essentially performed by hand, limiting how quickly it could be produced and making it an expensive commodity.

The first step toward a modern cocoa that could be enjoyed by all came in 1828 in Holland. In that year, a chemist by the name of Coenraad Johannes Van Houten patented a process that used a machine to squeeze most of the fat (cocoa butter) out of the cacao paste, resulting in a finer and more stable cocoa powder that could be produced cheaply and efficiently. (The cocoa butter, an expensive fat, could then be sold for use in other products.) To make the cocoa powder mix well with water or milk, Van Houten then treated it with alkaline salts (a process referred to as "Dutching"). The result was a smoother, less bitter cup of cocoa that was cheaper and more convenient for the consumer to prepare. Manufacturers soon discovered that the new cocoa powder could also be mixed with cocoa butter and sugar to form a thinner paste that in turn could be poured more easily into molds and would hold its shape once cooled. The modern chocolate bar was born.

These Industrial Age developments, along with the invention of milk chocolate (a process which will be explained in the following chapter), allowed for faster and cheaper production of milder forms of chocolate. For the first time in its history, chocolate was placed within reach of the common man, woman, and child. The rest, as they say, is history.

From Beans to Chocolate Treats

The way that cacao is grown and harvested today is little-changed from the days of the ancient Maya and Aztec. But modern technological advances have made it possible to process those beans into a rich assortment of affordable, flavorful chocolate treats that the original chocolate-makers could never have dreamed of.

As discussed in the first chapter, once chocolate arrived in Europe, its popularity only grew, as did the demand for the exotic beans from which it is made. Eventually, the craving for chocolate outgrew the ability of Mesoamerican sources to supply enough beans. So, to guarantee a sufficient, steady, inexpensive supply of cacao, the Europeans began establishing their own cacao-tree plantations in their colonies in the tropics: the British in Ceylon; the Dutch in Venezuela, Sumatra, and Java; and the French in the West Indies.

Today, very few of those large cacao plantations survive, mainly because chocolate-growers discovered that cacao trees are far more productive and hardy (without the use of expensive pesticides and chemical fertilizers) when grown in more natural surroundings and on a smaller scale that allows for more careful, hands-on tending. That's not really surprising, however, because cacao trees are quite delicate. They do well only under very specific temperature and moisture conditions (the cacao tree can only be grown in consistently hot and rainy areas within 20 degrees north or south of the equator), they require intensive cultivation, and their pods must be harvested by hand.

It is only when the cacao beans arrive at chocolate factories that technology can take over. Modern machinery and production methods, developed in the past 200 years, allow cacao beans to be processed into cocoa powder and all the other forms of baking, eating, or decorating chocolates that are available today.

On the Farm

Most cacao beans now come from small, independent cacao farms in tropical regions in Africa and Indonesia. On these small farms, the cacao trees are planted among taller trees, such as banana, rubber, and coconut. The taller "mother trees" shelter the cacao trees from harsh sunlight and wind, help limit the spread of diseases and pests, and ensure a steady supply of decaying leaves and other plant matter that naturally enrich the soil. That natural ground cover also provides habitat for the midges (tiny insects) that pollinate the cacao plants. The

Name That Plant

Despite the similarities in their names, the cacao tree (*Theobroma cacao*) from which chocolate and cocoa are derived is related neither to the coconut palm (*Cocus nucifera*) that gives us coconuts nor to the coca bush (*Erythroxylum coca*), the leaves of which are used to produce cocaine.

native farmers provide the intensive cultivation and diligent care necessary for the cacao trees to thrive and have the skill, experience, and patience required to handpick the beans and prepare them for market.

Growing and Harvesting Cacao Beans

Farmers raise cacao trees by first setting out cacao seeds in fiber baskets or plastic bags. It takes only a few months for the seeds to sprout and grow into seedlings that are then transplanted among the mother trees. In time, each seedling grows into a magnificent tree with large, glossy red leaves that gradually turn green as the tree matures. Although wild cacao trees can grow to a height of more than 50 feet, cultivated trees are usually in the 15- to 25-foot range. It usually takes a new cacao tree about five years to begin producing the fruit that holds the valuable cacao seeds.

Unlike most fruit trees in the United States, the cacao tree sprouts flowers and seed pods from its trunk and main branches. A typical cacao tree sprouts thousands of small, waxy, pink or white blossoms, although only 3 to 10 percent of these will eventually produce fully

The Life of a Tree

No one knows how long cacao trees can live, although a few individual trees have been recorded at more than 200 years old. In general, however, the productive life of a cacao tree is only about 25 years.

mature fruit. A healthy, productive tree can yield up to 2,000 pods a year. Another feature of the evergreen cacao tree is that it produces fruit year-round, so it is typically host to blossoms, unripened fruit, and fully mature seed pods all at the same time. The blossoms sprout from "cushions" that are clustered together on the trunk and main branches.

There are many varieties of cacao, and the trees cross-pollinate freely, but they fall into three basic types:

Criollo. The cacao considered to produce the best chocolate, criollo pods are soft and thin-skinned, with a light color and a pleasant aroma.

Forastero. The most common and easiest-to-cultivate variety, forastero cacao trees produce the most pods, which are thick-walled, have a pungent aroma, and produce a more bitter chocolate.

Trinitario. A natural cross of criollo and forastero, trinitario cacao blends the greater hardiness of the forastero tree with the milder and more aromatic flavor of the criollo beans.

The vast majority of chocolate today is made from the more bitter forastero variety, because forastero trees are hardier and produce more pods (making forastero beans cheaper) than the other two types. In recent years, however, cacao growers have been working on developing cacao hybrids to improve the quality and flavor of the beans while making the trees hardier and more resistant to disease. And recent interest in "gourmet" foods—especially among people who can afford to pay higher prices—has begun to increase demand for chocolates made from the rarer and more flavorful criollo beans.

Although cacao pods continually ripen on the trees, there are usually only two major harvests—sometimes with a third minor one in between—each year. It takes an experienced farmer to tell when cacao pods are ready for picking, and as in ages past, it takes careful manual labor to harvest them. Machines would simply cause too 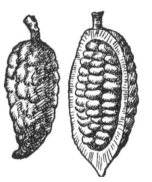 much damage to the trees. Ripe cacao pods must be individually handpicked to avoid harming the younger pods, tender blossoms, and delicate flower cushions (which will give rise to future pods) that are clustered with them on the trunk and main branches. In fact, the cacao tree is so easily damaged and its roots are so shallow that farmers don't dare climb it to harvest the ripe pods growing higher in the tree. Instead, the harvesters stay on the ground and use special long-handled cutting tools to snip off the higher pods. They deftly wield machetes to remove those closer to the ground.

Fermenting

Once the pods have been harvested and collected, they have to be opened—a task that itself requires skill and care to be done efficiently and without injury. Using a machete, an experienced cacao-farm worker can open up to 500 of the woody pods every hour without damaging the beans inside (or lopping off a body part). Once a pod is open, the whitish pulp, containing anywhere from 20 to 50 cacao beans, must be scooped out. (The edible pulp tastes sweet and lemony, but the cream-colored beans are far too hard and bitter to eat at this stage.)

The workers then pile up the pulp-coated beans and cover them with banana leaves or spread them out in long, shallow, covered wooden boxes to encourage fermentation to begin. Fermentation is a natural chemical process in which yeast, bacteria, or other microorganisms break down the sugar in the pulp into acidic compounds such as vinegar. The fermentation process is vital to the creation of chocolate, because it triggers chemical changes that help the beans develop their chocolate flavor.

Fermentation generates heat, causing the temperature within the pile of cacao beans to reach 120 degrees Fahrenheit or more. The heat, in turn, kills the germ of the bean (the part that would sprout and develop into a new plant) and liquefies the pulpy residue, which then just drains away. The heat also activates certain enzymes in the beans that tame their bitterness, form compounds that contribute to the chocolate flavor, and give the beans a brown color. Milder beans (such as the criollo variety) typically need to be fermented for only about three days, while more bitter beans (including forasteros) may require six to nine days of fermentation. Inadequate or interrupted fermentation prevents the development of true chocolate flavor. When the cacao beans finally turn brown, they are ready to be dried.

Drying
At this point, the fully fermented beans are typically spread out on bamboo mats or special trays and left in the sun to dry—a process that takes a few days to weeks. They are turned occasionally to help the process along and prevent mold from growing. At night, the beans are covered or brought indoors to keep dew from settling on them. If the weather is too damp during the day, the beans may be kept indoors and dried with hot-air blowers. Faster methods, such as drying the beans using the heat of a fire, are usually avoided because they can add unwanted flavors to the beans.

The drying step reduces the moisture in the beans, which decreases the risk of mold growth as the beans make their way to chocolate factories. But it is also during the drying stage that additional chemical changes occur that are essential to the development of the chocolate flavor of the beans. In addition, while the beans are laid out for drying, the farmer can pick through them to remove foreign particles and flat, broken, or germinated beans. By the end of the drying step, the beans have lost most of their moisture (usually at least 92 percent of it) and more than half their weight.

After drying, the beans are packed in sacks for shipment to the warehouses of commodity brokers. If the crop is approved, the buyers pay the farmer the current market price as set by cocoa exchanges (similar to stock exchanges) in New York, London, Hamburg, and Amsterdam. From the brokers' warehouses, the cacao beans are shipped to chocolate manufacturers around the world.

At the Factory

Once the beans arrive at the factory, they go through a fairly standard set of processing steps, with the number of steps dependent in part on whether the beans are destined to become cocoa powder or chocolate. Throughout this part of the journey from inedible bean to tasty treat, technology rules. In some manufacturing plants, computers are even used to run the machines and monitor the results to ensure the consistency and quality of the final products. Yet the modern machines and manufacturing processes have done more than make chocolate production faster and easier than in centuries past. They have actually redefined chocolate for the modern world, transforming the bitter, grainy, liquid chocolate of the ancients into the wide vari-

Bean Counting

Dried beans from an average cacao pod weigh less than two ounces, and it takes about 400 cacao beans to produce one pound of chocolate.

The Start of a Legend

Chocolate king Milton Hershey got his start in the business after discovering chocolate-making machinery at the 1893 World's Columbian Exposition in Chicago. Hershey began making chocolate-covered caramels that same year. He would go on to build a factory and a company town that carry his name and continue to flourish today in the quiet, rolling hills of southeastern Pennsylvania.

ety of rich, smooth candies, bars, cocoas, fillings, toppings, sauces, and flavorings that we know as chocolate today.

Processing the Beans

Chocolate manufacturers have their own proprietary recipes for making their various chocolate products. The vast majority of those products are made from specific blends of different types of beans. The secret recipes dictate exactly which types of beans, from which sources, and in what amounts, to use for each product. By following those recipes to the letter, the manufacturer can maintain quality and consistency in its final products.

When cacao beans arrive at the factory, therefore, they are carefully sorted and tracked according to type of cacao and plantation of origin. The beans are then cleaned by a machine that removes any remaining pod fragments, dried pulp, and other debris.

Next comes the all-important roasting stage. The future quality of the chocolate (or cocoa)—in terms of flavor, aroma, and appearance—depends on careful roasting. The beans are roasted as they tumble around in large, heated, rotating cylinders. Depending on the variety of bean and the desired result, the beans may be roasted anywhere from 30 minutes to 2 hours at temperatures of 250 degrees Fahrenheit or above. During roasting, their moisture content drops even further, their color deepens to a rich brown, and the characteristic aroma of chocolate develops.

Time Well Spent

It can take between two and four days to make one bar of chocolate.

After roasting, the beans are quickly cooled, leaving their thin shells dry, brittle, and easy to remove. The beans are then fed into a winnowing machine, where rollers crack the shells and fans blow away the shell fragments. What remain are pieces of cacao called "nibs."

At this stage, nibs from various types and sources of cacao are weighed and carefully combined (blended) according to each manufacturer's unique recipe. The specific blend used plays a major role in determining the flavor of the chocolate or cocoa that will result.

The blended nibs are next fed into mills, where they are ground into a paste. The process of crushing the nibs between large grinding stones or heavy steel discs produces heat, which liquefies the fat within the nibs. The fat in cacao is called cocoa butter, and the nibs consist of 54 percent cocoa butter. The resulting mash of liquefied cocoa butter and ground cocoa solids is known commercially as "chocolate liquor." (The name is a bit of a misnomer, though, because "liquor" here means liquid, not alcohol, yet the substance itself is actually more of a paste than a liquid.) All cocoa powder and chocolate products are made from this chocolate liquor. And it is at this point that the process for making cocoa powder and the process for making chocolate diverge.

Making Cocoa Powder

The beverage we call cocoa, or hot chocolate, in the United States is not the same as the hot cacao liquid consumed throughout most of history. The original "hot cacao" was made by combining water with ground cacao beans, which still contained all their natural cocoa butter. Since oil and water don't mix, the cocoa butter in the ground beans prevented the cacao from dispersing evenly in the water. The result was a thick, gritty beverage with a layer of oily fat floating on its surface—a far cry from the smooth and creamy cocoa we enjoy today.

Modern hot chocolate was born in 1828 in Holland. That's when chemist Coenraad Johannes Van Houten patented a process for removing much of the cocoa butter from ground cacao beans and then treating the resulting powder with an alkali substance such as baking soda to make it mix better with water. The alkali  treatment is referred to as "Dutching," in recognition of its origins, and the darker-colored, lighter-flavored cocoa that results is called Dutch cocoa.

To make Dutched cocoa powder, chocolate liquor is pumped into giant hydraulic presses, where about half of the cocoa butter is squeezed out. Baking soda is added to the remaining material, which is called "press cake." The treated press cake is then cooled, pulverized, and sifted to form cocoa powder. The cocoa powder is then packaged for sale in grocery stores as hot-chocolate mix or sold in bulk for use as a flavoring by dairies, bakeries, and candy manufacturers (the Dutching process makes the cocoa powder far more useful as a flavoring for other foods, as well).

The yellowish, liquid cocoa butter pressed out of the chocolate liquor does not go to waste. It is actually a very valuable commodity that, as described in the following section, is vital for manufacturing chocolate. Cocoa butter can also be sold—at high prices—to other manufacturers for use in pharmaceuticals and cosmetics.

Making Chocolate

While making cocoa powder is about removing much of the cocoa butter from chocolate liquor, making chocolate (the

Soldier's Helper

The popularity of the chocolate bar soared during World War I, when the U.S. government included chocolate bars in every soldier's ration kit as a quick energy-booster. Today, the U.S. Army continues to fortify its troops with rations of chocolate. Chocolate is also part of the diet of U.S. astronauts in space.

common eating varieties, at least) is about adding extra cocoa butter, as well as other ingredients, to the chocolate liquor. Cocoa butter is an absolutely essential component of chocolate. Indeed, it accounts for about 25 percent of the weight of most chocolate bars.

Cocoa butter has such enormous importance in the making of chocolate because of its unique qualities (which also make it valuable in pharmaceutical and cosmetic manufacturing). It is the only vegetable fat that is solid at room temperature, allowing for the production of chocolate "bars" and other molded chocolate candies. Cocoa butter is also unusual in that it melts at 89 to 93 degrees Fahrenheit—just below body temperature—and so is responsible for giving chocolate its melt-in-your-mouth appeal. Last but not least, cocoa butter resists oxidation and rancidity very well, allowing it to be stored at room temperature for years without spoiling.

A Chocolate-Lover's Dream Bar

The largest chocolate bar ever manufactured weighed 5,026 pounds and was exhibited by Elah-Dufour United Food Companies at Eurochocolate in Turin, Italy, in March 2000, according to *Guinness World Records*.

To make eating chocolate, then, additional cocoa butter is blended into chocolate liquor; depending on the type of chocolate being made and the manufacturer's recipe, sugar and other ingredients may be added, as well. The amounts of cocoa butter, chocolate liquor, and other ingredients are strictly dictated by the manufacturer's proprietary formula (and by government regulations, which are discussed later in this chapter). The ingredients are thoroughly mixed together, in some cases for hours. The mixture is then refined by being passed between heavy rollers (multiple times for the finest chocolates) to smooth out grittiness.

Next, the chocolate mixture is poured into a special shell-shape machine for a process called "conching." Conching was invented in 1879 by Swiss chocolate-maker Rodolphe Lindt and helped usher in the age of modern, velvety-smooth chocolate. Conching is a mechanical kneading process in which heavy rollers move back and forth through the chocolate mixture. The rollers agitate and aerate the chocolate, developing the chocolate flavor and further breaking down the chocolate and sugar molecules to make the chocolate silkier and more pliable. By carefully adjusting the speed of the rollers and level of aeration, the manufacturer can alter the chocolate's flavor and texture. In general, the longer chocolate is conched, the smoother it will be. Conching may be performed for as little as a few hours, although a high-quality chocolate may be conched for as long as three days. Additional cocoa butter may be added at this stage for a richer chocolate. A fat called lecithin, derived from soy, is often added as a stabilizer at this stage, too. And any additional flavoring ingredients, such as vanilla, that were not added earlier may be included at the conching stage.

Some manufacturers supplant or supplement the conching phase with a step called emulsifying. In this process, a sort of giant eggbeater breaks up the sugar crystals in the chocolate, resulting in a more velvety texture.

Before the chocolate can be poured into molds, dripped over fillings, or shipped off in liquid form to other food manufacturers, it needs to go through one more step, called tempering. Friction during the conching process naturally heats up the chocolate. During tempering, the chocolate is slowly, carefully, and repeatedly cooled and heated while being stirred continuously. Tempering is a stabilizing process that helps to keep the chocolate crystals from clumping together, which would give the chocolate a grainy or crumbly texture. It also gives the final product a smooth, glossy appearance and prevents the cocoa butter from separating out and causing a dull, grayish "bloom" on the surface of the chocolate. It's a complicated process that, done improperly, can seriously affect the quality of the final chocolate product.

Types of Chocolate

By using modern manufacturing processes and adjusting how much of what ingredients they add to the mix, chocolate-makers have been able to create a variety of chocolate "experiences" for consumers of all means. Manufacturers in the United States and Europe do, however, have to follow certain rules and regulations that define the basic types, or categories, of chocolate and dictate minimum levels of specific ingredients that must be present in these products.

Unsweetened, or Baking, Chocolate

Unsweetened chocolate (also called baking chocolate) is, essentially, pure chocolate liquor with no sugar added. It is "100% Cacao" and may be sold either Dutched or natural (without the addition of an alkalinizing agent). Because of its bitterness, this solid chocolate was traditionally sold for use only in baking, the assumption being that it would be added to recipes in which sugar was also an ingredient. Remarkably, though, manufacturers of today's finest chocolates have begun packaging it as an eating chocolate as well, marketing it as unsweetened "100 percent cacao content chocolate" in order to appeal to consumers seeking foods and flavors closer to their natural or unadulterated state. Chocolate connoisseurs who favor bittersweet chocolate may indeed savor the intense flavor of pure chocolate, but most people find it far too bitter to enjoy.

What Does "% Cacao" Mean?

The use of the "% Cacao" designation on chocolate wrappers began in Europe, where chocolates must have a label indicating the product's minimum total of cacao-derived ingredients, including chocolate liquor, cocoa butter, and cocoa powder. In France and Spain, the total amount of these three ingredients is stated as "% Cacao"; in Germany, it's "% Kakao"; and in the United Kingdom, it's "% Cocoa." In the United States, chocolate manufacturers are not required to declare the percentage of cacao in their chocolate products. However, as more Americans have become educated about quality chocolate and have sought out fine imported varieties that bear the designation, many American producers have begun listing "% Cacao." Some have also brought out their own lines of cacao-rich chocolate products.

Dark Chocolate

"Dark chocolate" is the general term used for chocolate that contains chocolate liquor—and usually additional cocoa butter, sugar, lecithin (as an emulsifier), and flavorings—but little or no milk. While there is general agreement that this term refers to chocolate that contains less than 12 percent milk solids, there seems little consensus on the minimum chocolate-liquor content required of the dark-chocolate category as a whole or of the individual varieties of chocolate within that category.  In Europe, for example, dark chocolate must contain at least 35 percent chocolate liquor and have a cacao content of at least 43 percent. In the United States, on the other hand, the government requires a minimum of only 15 percent chocolate liquor for this category. But here are some rough guidelines for understanding the varieties of dark chocolate that are available in the United States:

Sweet chocolate. This is the U.S. government's name for dark chocolate, and by legal definition, it must contain at least 15 percent chocolate liquor. The mildest dark chocolates typically have a cacao content of 15 percent to 34 percent.

Semisweet chocolate. This sweetened dark chocolate is often sold as "morsels" or "chips" for use in chocolate-chip cookies and other baked goods, although it can also be found in bar form. According to the U.S. Food and

Sweet Tip

The higher a chocolate's cacao content, or "% Cacao," the less sugar it contains.

Drug Administration, semisweet chocolate must contain a minimum of 35 percent chocolate liquor. Its cacao content is typically in the 35 percent to 49 percent range. Technically, semisweet chocolate contains a higher percentage of sugar (and therefore a lower percentage of cacao) than bittersweet chocolate does, but the terms are sometimes used interchangeably, and semisweet chocolate can be substituted when a recipe calls for bittersweet.

Bittersweet chocolate. Bittersweet chocolate is sweetened dark chocolate that, according to the U.S. government, must contain a minimum of 35 percent chocolate liquor. Most bittersweet chocolate bars have a cacao content of at least 50 percent, and some have a cacao content approaching 100 percent. As the "darkest" of the sweetened dark chocolates—the variety that has the highest cacao content—bittersweet chocolate has the most intense chocolate flavor.

Milk Chocolate

Milk chocolate, the most common eating chocolate in the United States today, actually arrived on the scene fairly late in the history of chocolate. Its development was made possible with the invention of powdered milk by Swiss chemist Henri Nestlé in 1867. Previous attempts at mixing whole (liquid) milk and chocolate liquor didn't turn out well. But in 1879, a Swiss chocolate manufacturer and neighbor of Nestlé by the name of Daniel Peter decided to try combining the newly invented powdered milk with chocolate liquor—and true milk chocolate was born!

Milk chocolate is made by combining chocolate liquor, cocoa butter, sugar, flavorings, and sweetened condensed or powdered whole milk (which one is used depends on the individual manufacturer's formula and production methods). The sugar and milk are first blended together, then they're mixed with chocolate liquor and flavorings and dried to create a substance called "milk chocolate crumb." Next, additional cocoa butter is blended with the crumb, and the mixture is sent through the standard conching and refining processes.

> ### It's a Western Thing
>
> Chocolate is not universally beloved. Asians, for example, seem far less bewitched by chocolate than are Westerners. The Chinese eat only one bar of chocolate for every 1,000 consumed by the British.

All milk chocolate made in the United States must contain at least 10 percent chocolate liquor and at least 12 percent milk solids. Bars of fine milk chocolate typically have a cacao content of between 30 percent and 45 percent, while less-expensive products may have considerably less. Milk chocolate has a sweeter and far more mellow chocolate flavor than dark chocolate, and since a higher cacao content gives a chocolate bar more "snap," milk chocolate tends to be less crisp than dark chocolate.

Dark Milk Chocolate

This newer variety of milk chocolate has a higher-than-usual percentage of cacao, giving it the deeper chocolate flavor of a semisweet bar along with the creamy smoothness of milk chocolate. The cacao content of dark milk chocolate is in the 45 percent to 70 percent range.

White Chocolate

Although white chocolate was introduced by the Nestlé company in the 1930s, the U.S. government did not create standards to define this category until 2002. In that year, the government required a product to contain a minimum 20 percent cocoa butter, at least 14 percent milk powder, and no more than 55 percent sugar to legally be termed "white chocolate" rather than a "confection."

Despite this new "definition of identity" from the government, white chocolate is not technically chocolate at all, because according to the established definition, a "chocolate" must contain chocolate liquor. Certainly, most chocolate connoisseurs, aficionados, and purists refuse to recognize it as anything but a candy or confection. (While it is sometimes referred to as "white milk chocolate," which is perhaps closer to the mark, even milk chocolate must contain at least

White-Chocolate Pretenders

Before the U.S. government established standards for white chocolate in 2002, many manufacturers of mass-market white chocolate substituted cheaper vegetable oils for some or all of the cocoa butter in their products, removing or severely reducing the only element in the mix that comes from cacao beans.

some chocolate liquor.) And as will be discussed in the next chapter, the lack of cacao solids (the nonfat part of the cacao bean) means that white chocolate is not likely to provide the health benefits of true chocolates.

The labels of some white chocolate bars do list a percentage, much the way the labels on true chocolates do, but this percentage does not refer to the percentage of cacao in the bar. Instead, it refers to the amount of cocoa butter. The higher the percentage of cocoa butter, the richer and creamier the bar and the more likely it is to have at least a hint of chocolate flavor.

Couverture, or Coating, Chocolate

This type of chocolate is a professional-quality product used for coating. It's made with higher-quality beans that are ground to a finer particle size and has a higher cocoa-butter content (usually 36 percent to 39 percent) than do chocolate bars for eating, giving it a texture and consistency better suited for use as a coating for candies. Couverture is specially tempered so it will form a thin, smooth, shiny coating on hand-dipped candies. The extra cocoa butter makes it easier for the artisan to use and allows the chocolatier to produce a more delicate coating, or shell, than would be possible with noncouverture chocolate.

Couverture chocolate is usually sold in 2.2-pound to 10-pound blocks for professional chocolatiers and chefs, but some companies also produce smaller-size blocks and wafers for use by the at-home candy maker.

A Flight to Quality

As many Americans have lately begun to refine their palates—opting for fine aged wines, 20-year-old balsamic vinegars, triple-virgin olive oils, and other "gourmet" food stuffs—they have started searching for superior chocolates, too. In response, gourmet chocolatiers have stepped up to meet the demand.

Like the other gourmet agricultural products mentioned above, chocolate benefits from intensive and careful cultivation but is vulnerable to variables such as weather and soil conditions. There are good years and bad for cacao-bean crops just as there are for the grapes used to make wine. Dif-

Single-Origin *vs.* Blended Chocolates

The typical chocolate bar is made from a combination of cacao-bean varieties (including criollo, forastero, and trinitario) that were grown in different regions and harvested at different times. It is therefore referred to as a blended chocolate bar. Blended bars may also be called "house bars," because they are blended using a consistent recipe year after year to represent the "house style" of the manufacturer.

The opposite of a blended bar is a single-origin bar, which is a gourmet chocolate made from beans that all come from the same area. It can either contain a blend or a single variety of bean, as long as the beans all come from the same geographic area—whether a specific island or a specific region, such as the Caribbean.

ferent producers in different regions can produce chocolates with startlingly different characteristics.

The emphasis of this new crop of gourmet chocolatiers is on producing smaller quantities of chocolate that contain extremely high-quality ingredients. Many pride themselves on the higher cacao contents of their products and/or the lack of pesticides and other chemicals used in the cultivation of their beans. While this flight to quality—to cacao-rich and responsibly grown chocolates—is certainly a happy trend for those who value gourmet goods, it is also a promising sign for people seeking to garner chocolate's health benefits, which are explored in the chapter that follows.

The high-quality chocolates from these gourmet chocolatiers tend to be sold in small shops, farmers' markets, and other off-the-beaten-path locations, as well as—increasingly—over the Internet. In another positive trend, however, the mass manufacturers of chocolate have been paying attention to consumers' shifting tastes and have themselves begun to create more affordable, higher-quality chocolates. More and more, even the lowliest grocery-store shelves are playing host to chocolates rich in the natural ingredients that may benefit our bodies as they tantalize our taste buds.

Chocolate's Healing Qualities

For years, chocolate has been looked upon as a decadent delight, craved for its lusciousness but banished to the "bad for you" food category. To the surprise of many health experts and the delight of chocolate-lovers everywhere, however, research has begun to reveal the healing potential hidden in the cacao beans from which chocolate is made. While these findings don't exactly elevate chocolate to the status of "health food," they do suggest that when it's chosen and enjoyed wisely, chocolate can have a place in a healing diet.

"If it tastes good, it can't be good for you."

How many times have you voiced a similar sentiment, shaking your head in exasperation at the injustice? You're not alone: Most people can tick off a list of favorite foods that fall into that category. For many of us, especially women, chocolate tops the list. Of course, that doesn't mean we don't eat chocolate. Indeed, its forbidden status may even add to its appeal. We keep hidden stashes of chocolate and nibble away in guilt or, worse, deny ourselves until desire overwhelms us and we gobble up giant bars of the stuff.

Fortunately, science has begun to chip away at chocolate's unhealthy reputation, exposing substances in cacao that have powerful healing properties. These properties don't negate chocolate's status as a high-calorie food, of course—especially the varieties most commonly consumed in the United States. And it's unlikely the latest research will prompt nutritionists and doctors to recommend that we add lots of chocolate to our diets. But the promising evidence of healing potential does suggest chocolate may no longer need to be forbidden fruit. Making room in the diet for limited amounts of cacao-rich chocolate and cocoa may thrill our taste buds, quench our cravings, *and* play a role in good health.

Many of chocolate's health-promoting properties appear to stem from special compounds, called antioxidants, found in cacao beans. So to explore chocolate's potential healing benefits, it's necessary to first understand how antioxidants function in the body and how they may protect us from disease.

Antioxidants: Our Radical Fighting Force

The antioxidant story begins with oxygen. We all know that oxygen is essential for life. Every cell in the body requires oxygen to get energy from nutrients. Without it, our bodies would simply shut down. Ironically, though, the very same oxygen molecules that keep us alive are easily turned into rogue particles that can leave a path of destruction throughout the body. The damage they cause sets the stage for a variety of diseases and, scientists suspect, prompts many of the changes we associate with aging.

How can something so vital become so harmful? When an oxygen molecule is in its normal, beneficial form, the electrons in its chemical structure are paired off. If that oxygen molecule loses one of its electrons, however, it becomes unstable—and destructive. This unstable molecule is called a free radical.

A free radical wants nothing more than to replace its missing electron, and it will steal one from wherever it can. If it robs a nearby oxygen molecule, that molecule becomes an unstable free radical. That destabilized molecule may, in turn, grab an electron from another molecule, causing a free-radical chain reaction. Alternately, an oxygen free radical may attack a nearby healthy cell, punching a hole in the cell's membrane to steal an electron and causing damage that may remain, even if the assaulted cell is able to replace its missing electron. The process in which oxygen free radicals assault stable molecules or healthy cells is called oxidation.

Free radicals can damage any tissue or organ, as well as any fat, protein, or carbohydrate molecule, in the body. The

Help Me—I'm Rusting!

The oxidation process is not unique to humans. In fact, it is the human equivalent of rusting. Metals form rust when their ordinarily stable molecules are oxidized. Other examples of oxidation include the browning of fruit when the flesh contacts air and the spoiling (rancidity) of cooking oils that eventually occurs once the airtight seals on their bottles have been opened.

"victims" may include DNA, the genetic material that regulates cell growth; the fat molecules in every cell's protective membrane; the low-density lipoprotein (LDL) molecules that carry cholesterol in the bloodstream; and the proteins that help form the structure of the heart, blood vessels, muscles, skin, and other tissue. Down the road, these kinds of insults may accumulate and lead to inflammation, abnormal or uncontrolled cell growth, hardening of the arteries, and other disease-inducing changes. Among the diseases thought to be associated with free-radical damage are coronary heart disease, cancer, emphysema and other lung ailments, Parkinson's disease, rheumatoid arthritis and certain other immune-system disorders, cataracts and macular degeneration, and Alzheimer's disease and certain other dementias.

How does an oxygen molecule lose an electron in the first place? Sometimes, the loss occurs during the body's normal use of oxygen for metabolic processes. In other words, some free radicals are simply natural byproducts of living. But far more often, exposure to environmental toxins such as air pollution, cigarette smoke, and the sun's ultraviolet (UV) rays results in the creation of free radicals.

Fortunately, our bodies have a natural defense mechanism against free-radical damage. The key element of that mechanism is a class of molecular compounds called antioxidants. Antioxidants neutralize free radicals, either by shielding healthy cells or by halting free-radical chain reactions. We have a number of antioxidant defenders at our disposal, each with its own protective functions. Some come in the form of vitamins and minerals. Vitamin C, vitamin E, and beta-carotene (a form of vitamin A) are antioxidants, as are the minerals selenium, manganese, and zinc. In addition, special chemicals from plants, called phytochemicals, can act as anti-oxidants in our bodies. We arm ourselves with these natural protective chemicals by eating a diet rich in plant foods, including vegetables, fruits, whole grains, legumes, and nuts.

Unfortunately, this anti-oxidant defense mechanism is not foolproof. It typically has little diffi-culty keeping up with the free radicals created by normal bodily functions, but it can be overwhelmed when we expose ourselves to too many environmen-tal toxins and/or don't replenish our antioxidant stores by regularly con-suming enough minimally processed plant foods (processing, as well as overcooking, tends to strip plant foods of some of their natural antioxidants). The resulting oxidative stress is thought to set the stage for the various diseases associated with free-radical damage. The good news is we can reduce our exposure to many environmental causes of free radicals. Plus, we can bolster our defenses against free-radical damage by boosting our dietary intake of antioxidants. That's where cocoa and chocolate can help.

Sharing Their Protection

Although phytochemicals help defend our cells from damage, that's not why plants produce them. Plants produce these chemicals to protect them-selves from predators, disease-causing organisms, and other environmental threats. We're just lucky we can share in their wealth of defenses.

Flavonoids: Cacao's Antioxidant Superstars

Researchers have discovered that cacao is rich in antioxidant phytochemicals, especially a type called polyphenols. Polyphenols are found not only in chocolate products but in fruits and fruit juices, vegetables, tea, coffee, red wine, and some grains and legumes. And the available research seems to strongly point to some role for polyphenols in preventing a variety of diseases.

The largest and most important class of polyphenols are the flavonoids. More than 5,000 flavonoids have been identified so far, and they have begun to attract a lot of attention for their potential health benefits. Among the flavonoid-rich foods that have shown promise lately are strawberries and blueberries, garlic, red wine, and tea. But these plant foods can't hold a candle to cacao-rich dark chocolate and cocoa products when it comes to flavonoid content and antioxidant power. Cocoa, for example, has almost twice the antioxidants found in red wine and close to three times the antioxidants in green tea, when compared in equal amounts.

One of the flavonoids in cacao (known as cocoa flavonoids, or cocoa polyphenols) gaining a particular reputation for healing is epicatechin. One Harvard Medical School scientist is so impressed by epicatechin's effects that he has said it should be considered essential for human health and, therefore, raised to the status of a vitamin. He's also stated that the health benefits of epicatechin are so striking that it may rival penicillin and anesthesia in terms of importance to public health.

The researcher developed his views on epicatechin after spending years studying the health benefits of heavy cocoa drinking on an isolated tribe of people called the Kuna, who live on islands off the coast of Panama. The Kuna drink up to 40 cups of natural (unsweetened) cocoa per person every week. The Harvard scientist, working with an international team of colleagues, found that the island Kuna have remarkably low rates (less than 10 percent) of four of the five most common killer diseases in the industrialized world: heart disease, stroke, cancer, and diabetes. The research further indicates that the Kuna's high intake of epicatechin from their cocoa is a primary cause of the low disease rates. Indeed, when tribe members leave their isolated islands to settle on mainland Panama—where they drink far less of the natural cocoa—their disease rates rise.

In addition to demonstrating the healing potential of cocoa, the Kuna research highlights an important point about that potential. The Kuna not only drink large quantities of cocoa, the cocoa they drink has a very high flavonoid content—far higher than the flavonoid content

Bold Is Healthy

Phytochemicals are often the substances responsible for the colors, aromas, and flavors of plants. So a bold appearance, strong taste, and/or pungent scent generally signals that a plant is rich in phytochemicals—and therefore loaded with antioxidant potential. When it comes to chocolate, the more of cacao's natural bitterness that remains in the product, the higher in phytochemicals (flavonoids) it tends to be.

of many of the sweetened, high-calorie, high-fat cocoa and chocolate products found on grocery-store shelves. And that's essential to its apparent health benefits. The Kuna grow their own cacao beans, gently roast and minimally process them, and use them to make an unadulterated cocoa that has a very high percentage of cocoa solids. And it's the cocoa solids that contain the flavonoids.

Flavonoids, however, also give natural chocolate a very bitter taste. So in an effort to please their sweet-toothed consumers, chocolate manufacturers have traditionally tried to tame that natural bitterness by removing flavonoids and/or masking their taste. (Fortunately, as you'll learn later in this chapter, that tradition may be changing somewhat.) Nearly every step of the typical processes that turn cacao beans into chocolate and cocoa—including fermenting, roasting, and Dutching— removes some of the flavonoids. Likewise, adding ingredients such as sugar and milk to chocolate or cocoa—again, to mask or replace bitterness—leaves less room for cocoa solids and therefore results in a lower-flavonoid product.

While the rest of us cannot control the way our cacao beans are grown and processed, as the Kuna do, we can increase our chances of getting and benefiting from cocoa flavonoids by opting for cocoa and chocolates with the most cocoa solids and the least sugar and milk added. You'll find advice on that later in the chapter. First, however, let's look at some of the studies that illustrate and support the specific disease-fighting effects of chocolate and cocoa.

Cocoa Flavonoids and Disease

A variety of studies, in addition to the research on the Kuna, have begun to illuminate how flavonoid-rich cocoa and chocolate may help fight serious disease.

Heart Disease and Stroke

In the past several years, scientists have produced some compelling research suggesting that cocoa flavonoids can help lower blood pressure, improve blood-vessel function, make blood less likely to form dangerous clots, and prevent the creation of artery-clogging blood-cholesterol molecules. All of these effects help ensure smooth, adequate, and uninterrupted blood flow to the heart and brain, lowering the risk of heart attack and stroke.

Blood Pressure. In a study published in August 2003 in the *Journal of the American Medical Association,* eating dark chocolate helped individuals lower mild high blood pressure, while eating white chocolate did not. The study included 13 men and women, ages 55 to 64, who had untreated mild high blood pressure. Each participant ate 90 grams of either dark chocolate or white chocolate each day for two weeks. Before the two-week experiment ended, those who ate the dark chocolate had significantly lower blood pressure, while the folks who ate white chocolate showed no such improvement. (Dark chocolate, you'll remember, contains chocolate liquor, made of cocoa solids and cocoa butter. White chocolate does not contain chocolate liquor and therefore provides no flavonoid-containing cocoa solids.)

In a similar study in Italy, published in 2005 in the journal *Hypertension,* researchers studied ten men and ten women who had high blood pressure. They were randomly assigned to eat either 100 grams of flavonoid-rich dark chocolate or 90 grams of flavonoid-free white chocolate each day for 15 days without increasing their total calorie intake (they were instructed to lower their calorie intake from other foods to compensate). Then, after a one-week break, they switched, with the subjects who previously ate dark chocolate daily now eating white chocolate, and vice versa, for another 15 days. The results: When the subjects ate dark chocolate, their systolic blood pressure (the upper number) dropped an average of 12 points and their diastolic pressure (the bottom number) dipped an average of 8. Eating white chocolate provided no such benefits.

Chocolate's Other Nutrients

Chocolate is also a good source of certain vitamins and minerals your body needs to stay healthy, including vitamins C, D, and E; B-complex vitamins; and the minerals iron, copper, phosphorus, zinc, calcium, and potassium. Cocoa is also the greatest natural source of magnesium, a deficiency of which is associated with high blood pressure, heart disease, diabetes, joint problems, and premenstrual syndrome.

And a 2007 review of ten different studies of chocolate's effects on blood pressure indicated that flavonoid-rich cocoa and chocolate can indeed have a place in a blood-pressure-lowering diet as long as the total calorie count of the diet stays the same. On average, chocolate products lowered systolic pressure by 4 to 5 points and diastolic by 2 to 3—enough to lower heart-disease risk by 10 percent and stroke risk by 20 percent. The scientists did note, however, that because the studies were short term, it's unclear if the same effects would occur with consumption of small amounts of chocolate over the long term.

Blood-Vessel Function. In studies that were published in the *Journal of the American College of Cardiology* in 2005 and in *Proceedings of the National Academy of Sciences* in 2006, researchers demonstrated that the flavonoids (specifically, epicatechin) in flavonoid-rich cocoa beverages trigger the production of a natural substance called nitric oxide. Nitric oxide, in turn, causes blood vessels to dilate (relax), allowing for smoother blood flow.

Flavonoid-rich cocoa may even benefit the compromised blood-vessel function of smokers, to the point of potentially reversing some of the vessel damage caused by smoking, according to a study published in the *Journal of Cardiovascular Pharmacology* in March 2007. In smokers, the activity of endothelial cells (cells lining artery walls) is reduced; this reduction in activity is an early signal of blood-vessel diseases such as hardening of the arteries (atherosclerosis). In the two-part smoker study, 11 healthy male smokers first drank a series of specially made flavonoid-rich cocoa beverages (provided by Mars candy company) containing 28 milligrams to 918 milligrams of flavonols, a subgroup of flavonoids. Two hours after they drank the beverage with 179 milligrams of flavonols, their blood-vessel function showed a 50 percent improvement. As they drank the cocoas with greater amounts of flavonols, the benefits increased. After they drank the cocoa with 918 milligrams, their cigarette-induced blood-vessel damage appeared to have been reversed to the extent that their blood vessels functioned as well as those of someone with no risk factors for cardiovascular disease.

The first stage of the trial was followed by seven days of drinking three daily doses of the special cocoa (for a total of 918 milligrams of flavonols each day) to determine if the benefits continued. The subjects' blood flow improved each day, and after taking a 306 milligram dose on day seven, their cigarette-induced damage had nearly been reversed once again. The study paper indicated that the level of improvement in blood-vessel function after seven days of consuming the flavonol-rich cocoa was similar to the improvements produced by long-term treatment with statin drugs. (The researchers also noted that these improvements caused by cocoa flavonoids did not appear to be the result of their antioxidant effects.) One week after the end of the study, however, the subjects' blood-vessel function had returned to prestudy levels, indicating that cocoa drinking would have to continue to sustain these benefits. The authors also noted that larger studies need to be done to confirm these very exciting findings.

In another study released in March 2007, scientists found that consuming eight ounces of special flavonoid-rich cocoa every day for six weeks significantly improved the blood-vessel health of people who were mildly obese. In the study, 45 mildly obese adults consumed either a flavonoid-rich, dark-chocolate cocoa mix sweetened with sugar; an artificially sweetened version of the same cocoa mix; or a placebo (control) mix made of sweetened whey powder. The artificially sweetened cocoa mix was associated with a 39 percent improvement in blood flow, and the sugared cocoa was linked with a 23 percent improvement. The placebo mix, however, *lowered* blood flow by 12 percent.

Blood Clotting. When the inner walls of arteries are narrowed by deposits of cholesterol and other debris, a blood clot can easily shut down the blood supply to the organ fed by the artery—leading to a heart attack, stroke, or other serious tissue damage. For that reason, many heart patients are prescribed a daily 81 milligram aspirin tablet, which thins their blood and helps prevent clots. In a 2002 study, scientists were astonished to find that drinking a flavonoid-rich cocoa drink could be just as effective as the aspirin at preventing clots. The research found similar reactions to both treatments in a group of 20- to 40-year-olds: Both the cocoa drink and the aspirin kept blood platelets from sticking together and forming clots. The researchers stopped short of suggesting that heart patients who have been prescribed a daily aspirin should drink cocoa instead. (And you should *NOT* stop taking any medication that has been prescribed for you without first consulting your doctor.) But for people at risk who can't take aspirin every day, it's possible that eating more flavonoid-rich foods could provide similar benefits.

Blood Cholesterol. Consuming saturated fat in food can increase total blood-cholesterol levels and, especially, levels of LDL cholesterol, the so-called "bad" form of blood cholesterol. Having too much LDL cholesterol is a risk factor for cardiovascular diseases, including heart attack and stroke, because LDL molecules tend to deposit excess cholesterol on the inner lining of artery walls, narrowing the arteries and setting the stage for a clot to cut off blood flow to the heart or brain. Scientists have discovered, however, that not all LDL molecules are equally damaging. It appears that LDL molecules that have been oxidized are the true culprits in clogging arteries. And that's where cocoa flavonoids may help. First, research suggests cocoa flavonoids may lower LDL levels. For example, in the 2005 study of Italians with high blood pressure, cited previously, the subjects who consumed flavonoid-rich dark chocolate experienced a 10 percent decrease in their LDL levels, in addition to a drop in blood pressure. Second, two 2001 studies showed that cocoa flavonoids can actually protect LDL molecules from oxidation.

In another bit of good news, scientists have determined that even the fat in cacao isn't so bad. Although cocoa butter is technically a saturated fat, it does not appear to increase LDL levels in the blood the way other saturated fats do. Half the saturated fat in cocoa butter is stearic acid, which studies indicate has a neutral effect on blood cholesterol. Chocolate also contains some oleic acid—the same type of mono-unsaturated fat found in olive oil, which can actually help lower LDL levels and boost levels of high-density lipoproteins (HDLs)—the "good" form of cholesterol that helps remove excess cholesterol from the blood.

Cancer

Study after study has demonstrated that a high intake of fruits and vegetables is associated with a reduced risk of several common cancers, such as those of the lung, colon, prostate, and breast. Scientists suspect that the reduction in risk comes, at least in part, from the antioxidants in those plant foods. Further, several laboratory, animal, and human studies point specifically to flavonoids as providing protection against cancer-promoting free-radical damage. And of the plant-based beverages known to be rich in flavonoids, Cornell University food scientists were amazed to find that cocoa contains the highest levels by far.

There is even some early evidence suggesting cocoa flavonoids may help fight skin cancer. In 2006, German researchers reported on their study of 24 women who  added cocoa to their breakfast every day for about three months. Half the women consumed a flavonoid-heavy hot cocoa, and the others drank a cocoa that had few flavonoids. At the end of the trial, the researchers applied

UV light—like that given off by the sun and found to cause skin cancer—to each subject's skin. The skin of the women who drank the high-flavonoid cocoa did not redden as much as the skin of the women who drank the flavonoid-poor cocoa, suggesting the flavonoids prompted some type of innate skin protection.

Diabetes

An emerging area of interest is the potential benefits of cocoa flavonoids for people with the most common form of diabetes, type 2. People with type 2 diabetes have become resistant to the effects of insulin, a hormone released by the body that escorts sugar into cells for use as fuel. As a result, damaging levels of sugar build up in the blood. Insulin sensitivity relies, in part, on nitric oxide. And some early evidence suggests that cocoa flavonoids may help decrease insulin resistance and improve blood-sugar control by increasing the availability of nitric oxide. (The positive effects of cocoa flavonoids on blood vessels and circulation would also benefit people with diabetes, whose nerves and blood vessels become damaged by years of exposure to high blood-sugar levels.)

According to the study of Italian men and women in which dark chocolate produced a decrease in both blood pressure and LDL cholesterol, eating 100 grams of dark chocolate every day for 15 days appeared to improve insulin sensitivity and lower blood-sugar levels, as well. Consuming flavonol-free white chocolate did not.

It should be remembered, however, that the study subjects lowered their intake of calories from other foods to compensate for the added chocolate in their diet. That's an essential point to reiterate when discussing the potential benefit of chocolate or cocoa in people with diabetes. Excess weight greatly increases the risk of type 2 diabetes, and any blood-sugar benefit that might be attained by consuming cocoa or chocolate would be easily negated by the excess weight gain that would likely occur if the chocolate calories were simply added to the diet.

Memory and Cognition

Cocoa flavonoids may act in more than one way to benefit mental performance, particularly in people with certain types of dementia. For example, free-radical damage and inflammation in the brain have both been cited as potential con-tributors to the memory problems and  cognitive decline that can occur with age and that are char-acteristic of dementias. We've already explored the amazingly powerful antioxidant effects of cocoa flavonoids. But these flavonoids also appear to suppress leukotrienes (substances that trigger inflammation in the body) and increase forms of anti-inflammatory nitric oxide.

In addition, the improvement in the health and function of blood vessels and the increased circulation that appear to result from consuming cocoa flavonoids may prove benefi-cial for those suffering dementia or other problems related to poor blood flow to the brain. In British research that was reported at the February 2007 annual meeting of the American Association for the Advancement of Science, drinking a flavonoid-rich cocoa beverage increased blood flow to key areas of the brain for two to three hours following ingestion. This increase in blood flow to the brain, scientists speculate, may be the result of greater amounts of nitric oxide in the circulation prompted by the cocoa flavonoids.

Some scientists are now considering the prospect of using cocoa flavonoids to help people with dementia and those who have had a stroke, as well as to enhance brain function in people suffering from fatigue, sleep deprivation, or poor circulation to the brain due to the aging of blood vessels.

Enjoying Chocolate Wisely

With such promising evidence of chocolate's healing potential, why *isn't* it considered a health food?

Despite the persistence of the myth, it's not because chocolate causes acne. It doesn't. (Although because we tend to reach for comfort foods when we're under stress, and stress *can* aggravate acne, it's an easy myth to believe.)

And it's not because chocolate is especially dangerous to teeth. Like any other carbohydrate, chocolate can indeed serve as food for oral bacteria, which excrete the acids that eat away at tooth enamel. But because it has a smooth texture and literally melts in your mouth, chocolate is actually a little less likely to cause cavities than are, say,  bread and other baked goods or candies such as licorice and caramel that tend to actually get stuck on or between teeth.

As long as you practice good oral hygiene and brush, or at least rinse, after eating chocolate, it's not a major danger to your pearly whites.

No, the reason health experts aren't pushing chocolate as a health food is the high calorie counts of commonly consumed chocolate products. There's no two ways about it: Chocolate is a relatively calorie-dense food to begin with, and the super-sweet, creamy, milky, high-fat versions so many Americans favor simply compound the problem. Such concentrated sources of calories could hardly be considered required eating in a nation battling overweight and obesity.

You Must Remember This

It takes 12 cacao beans to make one ounce of dark chocolate but only 4 to make an ounce of milk chocolate. The more beans, the more healing flavonoids; the higher the percentage of cocoa solids, the darker the chocolate; and the fewer the ingredients in your chocolate bar, the better it is for your health.

What's more, because so many folks find it so taste-tempting, there's a real concern that they'll find it difficult to moderate their consumption. The potential result is even more unwanted pounds. And those unwanted pounds would easily outweigh the health benefits described in this chapter. Overweight and obesity increase the risk of heart disease, stroke, diabetes, and some forms of cancer.

So, must you send chocolate, despite its healing powers, back to the forbidden-fruit category? No. As a matter of fact, making favorite foods totally off-limits can provoke feelings of deprivation that can trigger binging and other unhealthy eating habits, which can lead to the very weight gain you are trying to avoid. The better approach is to choose chocolate products that provide the most flavor and healing benefits for the fewest calories and then make room in your diet to accommodate them. It will take some effort—you'll need to check and compare labels to find the best calorie bargains—and self-discipline—you can't eat as much as you want without risking your health—but you'll be able to have your chocolate and keep your weight in check, too.

According to the government's Agricultural Research Service, when it comes to the common chocolate products that pack the most flavonoids and the greatest antioxidant punch, natural (rather than Dutched), unsweetened cocoa powders top the list. They also tend to be the lowest in calories and so can be the most weight-wise way to quench your chocolate desires. The process of Dutching, or alkalinizing, cocoa powder removes some of the natural flavonoids, so if you can  find it, choose an un-Dutched dark-chocolate cocoa powder (not a milk-chocolate cocoa mix), and prepare it with water. Sugar-sweetened powders retain fewer flavonoids—the sugar leaves less room for flavonoid-containing cocoa solids—and, of course, are higher in calories, so try an unsweetened powder (if you can't handle it unsweetened, you'll at least be able to add only as much sugar as is absolutely necessary) or, if you can find one, an artificially sweetened one.

When it comes to solid chocolates, opt for dark chocolates. Milk chocolates typically have no more than half the amount of cocoa solids that dark chocolates contain—and therefore they have far fewer healing flavonoids and much less antioxidant power. With the added milk and sugar, milk chocolate bars simply have far less room for cocoa solids and are often considerably higher in empty calories (calories that provide no nutritional benefit other than energy). A typical milk chocolate bar contains 30 percent cacao, 20 percent milk solids, 1 percent vanilla and emulsifier, and *49 percent sugar.* Some research even suggests that milk may interfere with the absorption of the antioxidants in cacao. And don't even bother with white chocolate if you're looking for any health benefits. It contains only cocoa butter, not cocoa solids (so no healing flavonoids), and loads of sugar.

These days, it seems, there's been an explosion in varieties and brands of dark chocolates. So how do you choose? Again, you want the products that are highest in cocoa solids. A helpful clue to cocoa-solid content is the "% Cacao" that is being listed on more and

Finally Getting Respect

With the growing interest in and evidence for the healing benefits of cocoa flavonoids, some chocolate manufacturers have begun developing ways to preserve more of cacao's natural flavonoids during the chocolate-making process.

more chocolates. It's not a guarantee of a hefty dose of cocoa solids, however. That's because the "% Cacao" refers not only to the cocoa solids but to the total percentage of ingredients that come from cacao beans, including cocoa powder and cocoa butter. But only the solids (including those within the cocoa powder) contain flavonoids. So even though two chocolate bars list "70% Cacao," for example, one can have fewer cocoa solids—and so fewer flavonoids—and more cocoa butter than the other. (The flavonoid content of a chocolate product may also be affected by such variables as the types of cacao beans used to create it, the soil and weather conditions those beans were grown in, the recipe and processing used, and the storage and handling of the finished product.) Still, in the absence of a label listing only the percentage of cocoa solids, it can be a helpful guide.

You'll also find useful information in the ingredients list and the Nutrition Facts panel. When comparing chocolates that have the same "% Cacao," look not only at the calorie counts but at which ingredients, other than those from cacao, have been added. Opt for the lowest-calorie product with the fewest noncacao ingredients.

How much chocolate and/or cocoa is it okay to consume? Moderation is absolutely key. If natural cocoa, especially an unsweetened variety, satisfies your taste for chocolate, that's definitely the way to go. You can probably enjoy a few cups a day. Because of its calorie content, however, you shouldn't look to add solid chocolate regularly to your diet unless you really enjoy it. If you do (and since you're reading this book, it's a good bet), you'll need to make room for it in your diet and then enjoy only as much as you've made room for.

That means that if you'd like to enjoy a square or two (but not much more) of cacao-rich dark chocolate every day, you'll need to cut back—by an equiva-  lent number of calories or more—on other sugary or fatty foods you eat that day. (If you're also trying to lose weight, you'll need to cut back even further on other sources of empty calories and, preferably, increase your physical activity level, too.) Do not replace nutrient-rich foods, such as veg- etables, fruit, and whole grains, with chocolate. That would truly be shooting yourself in the foot. Instead, cut back on foods such as sugary, high-fat baked goods; ice cream; fatty dressings and sauces; salty, greasy fast foods and snack foods; sweetened sodas; and other types of candy.

Once you've made room in your daily diet, make time to truly enjoy your chocolate. Take a few moments, sit down, and slowly savor the deep, rich flavor and melt-in-your- mouth texture of a high-quality dark-chocolate square. And remind yourself that there's no need to feel guilty about satis- fying your chocolate desires in a responsible, healthy way.

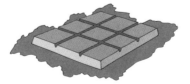